She Wears Her Crown

~ 31 Days of Self-Empowerment and Daily Declarations ~

A personalized women's devotional to help you evolve keep you encouraged and empowered.

Shirine Mcrae-Freeman

She Wears Her Crown

31 Days of Spiritual Empowerment and Declarations

She Wears Her Crown

31 Days of Spiritual Empowerment
and Daily Declarations

Author
Shirine Mcrae - Freeman

This page was left blank intentionally.

ACKNOWLEDGEMENT

A heartfelt thank you to my husband, Darius Freeman, parents and siblings for your continued prayers and support.

You have each touched my life and has helped me to become an honorable woman of strength.

My life has been deeply impacted by my spiritual family. Thank you for the encouragement you have poured into me over the years.

Copy Editor: Alyscia McRae-Fraser
Website: Shirinefreeman.com
Facebook: Freeman Transformation Academy
Instagram: Freeman Transformation Academy
ISBN: 9780578889801

FOREWORD

She Wears Her Crown

The significance and impact of advice or counsel that is based on learning from written work or from sitting under the tutelage of someone, pales significantly when compared to counsel, advice, or teaching that is borne out of personal experience. We live in an era of information overload; therefore, it is quite easy to obtain information and with some adjustment present it to others with an unjustified sense of authority.

When people give counsel that is a product of their own experience, they have an inherent right to speak from the place to which their experiences have taken them. These personal experiences mold the individuals from one level of maturity and functioning to another, and naturally prepare them to speak from their heart. Messages with this authentic foundation change lives.

I have watched Shirine Freeman grow from being a quiet, shy-looking young lady with a nervous-looking smile who could sit through a discussion of almost any length without saying a single word to a bold and confident young woman with a voice. She is now a woman who is assured in her calling and the anointing of God the Father on her life. She now embraces her purpose and with the release of She Wears Her Crown, seeks to bring as many sisters as possible along with her. This is a message with authority that you can glean from.

I want you to consider this 31-day devotional a tall glass of your favorite drink. This is not a drink you gulp down in a hurry. You must sip it slowly and savor the taste. I invite you to take a sip from this fountain of life for the next 31 days and watch the you inside of you emerge. Many blessings await you. Drink on!

Rosemarie Downer, Ph.D.

Author

TABLE OF CONTENTS

INTRODUCTION

She wears her crown was birthed from a place of me uncovering my purpose and rediscovering the God who knew me before I came into this world. Everything I am and will ever be, I owe it to the one who has crowned me with His glory and calls me his beloved. Maybe you were brought into the kingdom but unsure of the authority and power that are now available to you. Well sis, grab yourself a seat because your crown is about to sparkle. This book was written from biblical truths because only the Word of God has the power to overturn the lies you've been told. You are royalty.

For the next 31 days, allow Holy Spirit to take you on a journey of uncovering who you were always meant to be. No other force in the universe has the drive or power to bring to light who you are and why you are. It takes the one who created you to give insight on how you function and what you possess.

As you take this journey of self-discovery and in some areas, God discovery, embrace the fact that you were meant for everything royalty.

Life's experiences may have caused you to dim your shine and have tempted you to take off your crown but to pursue purpose as you uncover your power and authority is to wear your crown.

~ DAY ONE ~

She Knows no Boundaries

To discover the woman you were always meant to be, seek out the depths and heights of her, stopping at nothing. I pray you will jump over hurdles and find your inner beauty with childlike faith. Take a moment and live because in this space of royalty, you are not just breathing but living.

Let these words from your Heavenly Father penetrate your heart and cut asunder the lies of your soul. *He knows what He's doing! He has it all planned out!* His plans are to take care of you, not abandon you, and give you the future you hope for in Him.

She Declares

Today I release every thought that exalts itself above God's plans for my life. I lay down every false belief, action and habit which separate me from my Heavenly Father. I am more than enough and possess all that I need to live in abundance. I am free from rejection, guilt, fear and deception. I choose to embrace the revelation of God's Word over my life. I have been redeemed by the blood of Jesus and therefore operate from a place of authority and power!

She Meditates

“For I know the thoughts I have for you,” says your Father, “Thoughts to elevate you and give you what you should rightfully possess as my child." (Emphasis added) Jeremiah 29:11

She Journals

~ DAY TWO ~

Walking with Angels

The LORD declares His banner of provision and protection is over you. Embrace your status and power to walk high in His presence. Know that you are guarded by an army ready to defend your honor; angels have been given commands to catch you. They lift you up when all seems lost and catch you when your world may seem to cave in. They have been charged by your Father to hold you up. Yes! Supernatural beings are walking with you and are always ready to give a helping hand. In your waking hours and during your night rest, you are guaranteed protection!

Sis, did you know as an ambassador of God's kingdom you have guards? Yes, you are not only provided for but protected.

She Declares

I embrace the protection provided for me today by the angel army. I boldly acknowledge the presence of God walking with me today! No assignment of the devil will prosper over me because I abide in the light of God's Word. I am safe and I put off every influence of fear. Angels are at my disposal today, therefore, even if I fall, I will be caught before I hit the ground.

She Meditates

For He will command His angels in regard to you, to protect *and* defend *and* guard you in all your ways [of obedience and service]. Psalm 91:11 AMP

She Journals

~ DAY THREE ~

Excellence and Grace

Know that your qualities qualify you. If you are married, honor your husband. Be respectful to him as he functions in his role. Extend care and compassion to those who support you. You must endeavor to be governed by a disciplined life and be known to be a reliable daughter of the King. Strive to do your best as you show up in all your roles. When entering a room, let your poise and excellence be seen. Be frugal and wise in your spending. Consider stocks and real estate then buy them. Always ensure your household is cared for and lacks nothing.

She Declares

I am frugal in my doings and I know no poverty. I consider stocks and real estate and I invest wisely. I attend to the needs of my husband and children. I am careful to be on time and accomplish my day's tasks with grace and zeal. I show up as the godly woman and wife I've disciplined myself to be.

She Meditates

An excellent woman [one who is spiritual, capable, intelligent, and virtuous], who is he who can find her? Her value is more precious than jewels *and* her worth is far above rubies *or* pearls. Proverbs 31:10 AMP

She Journals

~ DAY FOUR ~

Standing on my Knees

Take the opportunity and dare yourself to believe on-your-knees for the stars that seem to be out of reach. Though your womb may appear to be barren, you have what it takes to defy the odds. Elevate your thoughts beyond the doctor's report. Stare the naysayers in their eyes and trust God for the changes you desperately longed for. The prayers you continually send up to heaven welcome God into your space, allowing the potter to shape you. You are a lady! Not only do you walk in stilettoes but on water too. Know that you are tallest when on your knees.

She Declares

I am strong and confident. My words and actions reflect soundness of mind, love and power. The spirit of fear has no influence over my thoughts and emotions. My will power, thoughts and emotions are healed and free from lies. Peace and calm overshadow my soul.

She Meditates

For God has not given us a spirit of fear, but one of power, love and sound mind. 2 Timothy 1:17 NKJV

She Journals

~ DAY FIVE ~

Unveiling Truth

Today, spend time with yourself, take a journey to strip away those layers of lies which formed your beliefs of who the devil wants you to think you are. Give yourself permission to tear down beliefs of perfectionism, rejection, hate and doubt. The lies you've inherited from your environment and previous generations have caused you to conform to the false image you've created. Those lies have dimed the shine in your crown tempting you to take it off.

She Declares

I declare that I have a Father and I am loved by Him. I am flawed but in Christ, there is nothing wrong with me. I release all lies of rejection and self-doubt in the name of Jesus. The word of God says I am God's creation and was made in His image. Therefore, I have the mind of Christ. My market value is the blood of Jesus. I redirect my attention to the face of Jesus as I walk the path of purpose wearing my crown. Confidently dressed in the power and authority He has given me.

She Meditates

But you are a chosen people, a royal priesthood, a holy nation, God's special possession, that you may declare the praises of Him who called you out of darkness into His wonderful light. 1 Peter 2:9 NIV

She Journals

~ DAY SIX ~

Fixing my Crown

Refresh your thoughts through the meditation of the Word of God. Sometimes life is uncertain and the unknown feels scary. Taking one step in front the other as you submit to your king guarantees your success. Yes, your crown may shift with distractions but regaining your focus is always key to getting back on track. This sphere of influence granted to you is used to empower who you are called to be.

She Declares

I will fulfill God's plans for me. I will walk in the light of God's word. I decree and declare that distractions, be it extrinsic or intrinsic, have no hold over my precious life. They are vetoed by the blood of Jesus. I am a source of blessings for those who I am called to.

She Meditates

For though the righteous falls seven times they rise again, but the wicked stumble when calamity strikes. Proverbs 24:16 NIV

She Journals

~ DAY SEVEN ~

Unapologetically Me

God has relocated you so that you can be found in Him. As you walk in the light of His word, focus on the prize. Those old habits have to go. He is creating a new wine skin, equipping you to carry His Spirit and function effectively in His kingdom. Stay true to your purpose as He makes himself known to you. Respond to life differently as you take hold of your true identity and launch out with love, power and soundness of mind.

You are being watched by many as they observe your new skin. You are here to influence change as God pours new wine into you. Some will not understand the transformed you because their foggy eyesight and mental limitations cannot comprehend your mission.

She Declares

I've been delivered from every oppressing spirit in the name of Jesus. I am not a slave to the words and actions of men but have been risen with Christ to live at my full potential. I am entitled to everything God has for me therefore, I keep my eyes steadfast on my reason for being a resident in His kingdom.

She Meditates

Neither do people pour new wine into old wineskins. If they do, the skins will burst; the wine will run out and the wineskins will be ruined. No, they pour new wine into new wineskins, and both are preserved. Matthew 9:17 NIV

She Journals

~ DAY EIGHT ~

Pressing for the Prize

Misdiagnosed actions and words misunderstood,
reaching beyond discomfort to attain the prize you should.
No retreat, no surrender, upward only you must climb.
Broken patterns and circles; shedding, breaking - redefined.
People removed, mindsets replaced;
once aborted the mission but made it by His grace.
Thoughts and emotions submitted to God,
nothing recycled, oh the heavenly applaud!
To operate from here, they are tests you must face,
but make it you will, only by His grace.

She Declares

Though troubles may come, I will remain faithful in my walk. I declare that I will look to God and depend only on Him to keep my thoughts and my life aligned in purpose. I declare that when my assignment gets tough, I will cry to God because my help comes from Him.

She Meditates

I press on toward the goal to win the prize for which God has called me heavenward in Christ Jesus. Philippians 3:14 NIV

She Journals

~ DAY NINE ~

You've evolved

You've pushed through your false beliefs and unlearned the lies which held you captive for so long. You've been introduced to new patterns, a new mindset and a new environment which facilitates your growth. Your authenticity is the result of the work you've put in. You've given yourself space and stripped away those layers of your identity that have been formed by circumstances. You've allowed yourself to capture the eternal beauty deposited in the many facets of your soul and ah, you've evolved. An apology for your wings isn't necessary. Not everyone is invited into this space; your algorithm has shifted. Elevated expectations viewed as isolated disconnection but the treasures of your evolution will remain a mystery to those of yesterday.

She Declares

Today I boldly embrace the transformation God is making in every aspect of my life. I surrender to the changes and open my mind to all things new. I will operate in what is good, what is righteous and what is pure in God's eyes.

She Meditates

So here's what I want you to do, God helping you: Take your everyday, ordinary life, your sleeping, eating, going-to-work, and walking-around life and place it before God as an offering. Embracing what God does for you is the best thing you can do for Him. Don't become so well-adjusted to your culture that you fit into it without even thinking. Instead, fix your attention on God. You'll be changed from the inside out. Readily recognize what He wants from you, and quickly respond to it. Romans 12:1 MSG

She Journals

~ DAY TEN ~

Bloody Knuckles

Keep knocking even when failing hurts your knuckles. Failing well means you have learnt the lessons and have decided to try a better way. Your disappointments don't define you and you're not a failure. Sometimes the door to success will open as it finds you with bloody knuckles. This is because you've decided to never give up on you and your destiny. No matter how challenging, keep knocking and if no one opens the door for you, build one. We live in a world where everyone is flashing their successes on social media but not much of their 'down' days. If we're not careful, we may allow the world's definition of success to fade us out of knocking on our own doors. Failing well becomes the deciding factor for a better approach. No matter what, keep fighting the good fight because there is a crown waiting for you.

She Declares

My job is blessed. My finances are blessed. My children are blessed. My marriage is blessed. My health is blessed. My possessions are a blessing and at all times I will bless the name of the living God.

She Meditates

Blessed be the Lord, my Rock, who trains my hands for war, and my fingers for battle. Psalms 144:1 ESV

She Journals

~ DAY ELEVEN ~

Heartbreaks

Maybe you've suffered from a broken heart through loss, divorce or death. Take some time for you to uncover your strengths and remind yourself that you are royalty. The internal feelings can create a shattered view of God's presence but the King is right there with you. Some questions may go unanswered and many things we may never understand now but if we remain still; we will see His hand writing all over the walls of our lives. Yes, He still heals our broken hearts.

She Declares

I am seated in heavenly places with Christ and there are no sicknesses in heaven. Therefore, healing is mine. I am a benefactor of heaven. I am enough, I am whole. I walk in excellence and open my heart to the comforting hands of Almighty God. I declare that no weapon formed against my trust in God shall prosper.

She Meditates

He heals the broken hearted and binds up their wounds. Psalms 147:3 ESV

She Journals

~ DAY TWELVE ~

Stewardship and Stilettoes

How you invest your time will result in what you reap. Plant seeds which gives you a harvest and change the direction of your future. Though you may not reap it immediately, harvest will come. You are not returning to unproductive habits you once held close. No longer will you obey the voices of yesterday telling you it's impossible. There may be some unexpected turns in life but slide on those stilettoes because today you are moving forward. Whatever you lack, ask God for an increase. Whatever He has trusted you with, allow it to multiply and serve others. That's how you'll honor your King in return. What has He given to you and how are you managing it?

She Declares

I will honor God by using the gifts, skills and talents he has given to me. I will spend money wisely as I save and invest. I will esteem others higher than myself as I allow God's love to manifest through me. I will pursue peace as much as possible with those I encounter. I will be a godly example to my children and other women. I will use my time wisely and allow my possessions to be a blessing to others. I will eat healthy and care for my body. I will not bury what my King has given me but facilitate its multiplication in every aspect.

She Meditates

Do not be deceived, God cannot be mocked. A man reaps what he sows. Galatians 5:16 NIV

She Journals

~ DAY THIRTEEN ~

Deliverance from Poverty

Poverty is a mindset manifested in the way we respond to life experiences. Many associate poverty with a sense of shame but this is a trap of the enemy to keep you hiding. While a person who is financially challenged may experience lack, that individual can be wealthy in other areas. On the other hand, one can be set financially yet possess a poverty mindset. Financial flow is only a small percentage of wealth. To unlock your wealth and break free from restrictions you must be willing to do the work. This is done by unlearning some inherited lies and educating yourself through various resources. Change the narrative of your bloodline. What are you willing to do to leave a legacy for the generations ahead of you? Weren't you brought to the kingdom for such a time as this? The ability to have what you need when you need it is an expression of wealth. What has God given you and what have you done with it?

She Declares

I am a child of the King; therefore, I know no lack. I declare that my mind is renewed by the Word of God. I decree that the spirit of poverty has no hold on my mind. I manage effectively my money, business, relationships, job, marriage, ideas, skills and talents from a place of wealth and freedom. I have a right to walk in wealth in every area of my life. I will do everything in my power to increase what God has given to me.

She Meditates

For if thou altogether holdest thy peace at this time, then shall their enlargement and deliverance arise to the Jews from another place; but thou and thy father's house shall be destroyed: and who knoweth whether thou art come to the kingdom for such a time as this? Esther 4:14 KJV

She Journals

____

____

____

____

____

____

____

____

____

____

____

____

____

____

____

____

~ DAY FOURTEEN ~

The Birthing Room

The shedding of the old is never easy as it requires a secret place. It calls for patience and pursuit. Welcome to the birthing room. It is a place of vulnerability where all are not invited. Those who are willing to lay down their perspectives, traditions and self-made platforms will push out what is unprecedented. Preparation will cost you everything as you willingly pay the price for your oil to flow. Your internal processing will rapidly produce a finished print after each exposure in God's presence. Not everyone is meant to be in the birthing room but you are here because in you lies a wellspring of ideas, creativity and solutions.

She Declares

I will not return to what God has delivered me from. I will carry and bring to full term every idea, every action and every assignment. I will not abort anything God has given to me. I will depend on Holy Spirit who will teach me, comfort me and nurture me in every season.

She Meditates

Very truly I tell you, unless a kernel of wheat falls to the ground and dies, it remains only a single seed. But if it dies, it produces many seeds. John 12:24 NIV

She Journals

~ DAY FIFTEEN ~

Give it Time

When my husband bought me a beautiful bouquet of roses, most of them were still in bud form while others were blooming. A quick trim and some water and I began to enjoy the fullness of their beauty. Watching them bloom reminded me of how rewarding waiting can be. What have you been waiting on to emerge? Is it taking longer than you expected? Do you feel less productive than those around you? Keep watering your vision and it will grow like the most beautiful flowers you've ever seen. Others may be getting there before you but never measure your path by using someone else's' measuring stick. Stay focused, you will get to the finish line.

She Declares

I will wait on the right time for the right things. I will push pass my impatience and rely on God to keep my mind. I will not allow frustration to take over my will and emotions. I will wait on the Lord because His timing is best.

She Meditates

But they that wait upon the LORD shall renew their strength; they shall mount up with wings as eagles; they shall run, and not be weary; and they shall walk, and not faint. Isaiah 40:31 KJV

She Journals

~ DAY SIXTEEN ~

Where are you going?

I had a daily routine established for myself. Even when life became unproductive following said plans, I maintained a "stick to it" attitude. I wanted to discover new things outside of my safe boundaries. I wanted my territory enlarged and my borders widened. Sadly, though, my daily routines had me going in circles. Then it hit me; I was passing by the same scene.

Routines aren't bad; they actually help us stay on track. If, however, the track becomes barren, it's time to rebel. You know where you are and where you want to be; it's the 'in between' that seems challenging. How can we connect ideas to reality? The journey requires a plan. That plan is your personal bridge to getting you to your destiny. It's easy for us to accept life as it comes but if we want to change our scenes, we must rebel against our safe established boundaries. We're either going somewhere or we're going around in circles.

She Declares

My steps are established by God because I find pleasure in chasing after Him. I will not lean on my own intellect, emotions and thoughts but seek out His direction for my life.

She Meditates

Trust in the Lord with all your heart, and do not lean on your own understanding. In all your ways acknowledge Him, and He will make straight your paths. Proverbs 3:5-6 ESV

She Journals

~ DAY SEVENTEEN ~

Kick Buts

Today we're kicking BUTS and setting our abilities free from our limiting beliefs!!! Like they say, we go big or we go home. As a woman, wife, and business owner I've doubted myself more than I would like to remember. The day I launched my own business, I was literally shaking. A few days later after revisiting the blueprint, I thought, "I'm great at managing MY finances and working on MY credit score BUT what if it's different for others?" Truth is, the strategies I use for mine and yours are the same. My BUT was in my way. There were times I procrastinated because the idea of greatness overwhelmed me. I wanted it BUT... I thought of doing it BUT... It's time to kick BUTS! What are your future plans? What's stopping you? Chances are, it's just YOU.

Today I challenge you to get out of your way. I know it can be hard, especially if you've tried but didn't achieve the expected results. So what? It was an experience that taught you what will not work the next time you try. Get off your BUTS and maximize your current abilities. You Got This!

She Declares

I will stand in confidence as I establish in my purpose. I declare that I will implement solutions instead of excuses. I walk in the spirit of excellence and laziness is far from my dwelling. I am brave, I am courageous, I am the king's daughter; therefore, I see only possibilities.

She Meditates

I can do all things through Christ who gives me strength. Philippians 4:13

She Journals

~ DAY EIGHTEEN ~

Next Level

Getting to the next level will demand the 'next level' thinking patterns. Where your thoughts go, your actions will follow. Are you waiting on the perfect weather or day of the week to experience change? Start with what you have and where you are. We serve a faithful king so let us walk by faith and not by what we see. Can you see God in your circumstances? Where is your focus? Allow your thoughts to soak in what God says about you. This is the first ingredient of the recipe to transformation. Esther had courage while Moses had a rod. Their internal views were challenged yet they did not allow what they saw to alter what they knew. Esther fasted three days then she approached the king and made her request known. Moses stretched forth his rod and his faith towards the sea and a way was made. Go ahead, approach every aspect of your life in faith and you will walk on dry ground.

She Declares

I decree and declare that my thoughts are in alignment with the Word of God. I decree and declare that my meditation is on things that are beautiful, praiseworthy and honest.

Today my mind is shifting and I now walk by faith and not by what I see.

She Meditates

Summing it all up, my friend, I'd say you'll do best by filling your mind and meditating on things which are true, noble, reputable, authentic, compelling, gracious—the best, not the worst; the beautiful, not the ugly; things to praise, not things to curse. Put into practice what you have learnt from me, what you heard and saw and realized. Do that, and God, who makes everything work together for your good, will work you into His most excellent harmonies. Philippians 4:8 MSG

She Journals

~ DAY NINETEEN ~

Intentional Moves

Decisions can be powerful. **The word *decide* means to come to a resolute in the mind.**

Approach your hour, day, week, month and year with intentionality. Whatever you choose to do is what you are deciding to do. Your decisions will affect the world you are creating for yourself and those around you. What decisions do you need to sow today so that your reaping tomorrow will be bountiful? Be deliberate and plan your decisions in advance. This way you are not caught off guard and your moves will return interest.

She Declares

I declare that there is clarity in my decisions based on God's direction for my life.

I decree and declare that I walk in the fear of the LORD which is the beginning of wisdom.

She Meditates

This book of the law shall not depart out of thy mouth; but thou shalt meditate therein day and night, that thou mayest observe to do according to all that is written therein: for then thou shalt make thy way prosperous, and then thou shalt have good success. Joshua 1:8 KJV

She Journals

~ DAY TWENTY ~

Self-care

Mental exhaustion can take a toll on the body if we do not stop, drop and roll. It is an internal fire that needs to be extinguished. Stop; say no, relax, breathe, go to bed earlier than usual, go for a walk, let them have cereal for dinner, enjoy your favorite dessert alone. Drop- all that can be dropped including laundry, grocery shopping and ministry work. (Be sure to contact your ministry leader first) Finally, roll. Roll yourself into the peaceful care of God where your mind is enveloped by perfect peace. Roll yourself into bed or into the bath tub for a moment of relaxation. You're not being selfish but wise. We cannot give the best of ourselves if we do not give ourselves the best that we truly deserve. Stop feeling guilty for taking care of you. In this kingdom queens get pampered too.

When you care for your mind, you care for everything else with the right attitude. You were not created to always be on the go or give your whole self to everyone, every time. Go ahead, create boundaries and take care of you.

She Declares

I decree that I will honor the temple of God which is my body. I place value on my body, soul and spirit because I was bought with Jesus' blood. I will not allow myself to be overwhelmed by what is external but create healthy boundaries to sustain a healthy internal view.

She Meditates

Do you not know that your bodies are temples of the Holy Spirit, who is in you, whom you have received from God? You are not your own; you were bought at a price. Therefore, honor God with your bodies. 1 Corinthians 6:19-20 NIV

She Journals

~ DAY TWENTY-ONE ~

Dollars and Sense

Since the Garden of Eden, we were given the opportunity to manage what God has entrusted to us. We are to steer everything we have into the direction of honor and multiplication. This includes our finances, skills, talent, time, wealth, gifts, children, and so on. Do not allow fear to bury what you carry. When your king returns He will be looking for interest. Multiply!

She Declares

I declare that I will be frugal and manage money wisely. I declare that I will invest my time and talent for the establishment of God's kingdom. I declare that I gain interest on my investments.

She Meditates

And unto one he gave five talents, to another two, and to another one; to every man according to his several abilities; and straightway took his journey. Then he that had received the five talents went and traded with the same, and made them other five talents. And likewise he that had received two, he also gained other two. Matthew 25:15-17 KJV

She Journals

~ DAY TWENTY-TWO ~

Heels and Crowns

Never stop uncovering the beauty of who you were created to be. That journey includes discovering hard truths and unlearning some beliefs about people, God, your past, present and future. The hike to authenticity is the process of stripping away layers of your identity that have been formed by everything but God. It is the process of tearing down expectations and false beliefs which had you bound to an image you have created.

It's time to take back the power you've given to people who viewed you based on what they know or think they know about you. You may not realize it but when you show up based on people's perspective of you, you re-empower their views. This is your time to transform and you deserve to shine as brightly as you possibly can. No longer will you hang on negative self-talk, people's opinion, a stagnant circle of friends or procrastination. Walking taller than before, she wears her crown.

She Declares

Today I take responsibility for my feelings/emotions, thoughts, actions, finances, relationships, spiritual development and personal goals. I am not afraid of standing tall. I am not afraid of walking in my true self. I am comfortable with me and confident that God will complete what he has started in me.

She Meditates

So God created man in his own image, in the image of God He created him; male and female He created them. Let God reconstruct your image. Genesis 1:27 KJV

She Journals

~ DAY TWENTY-THREE ~

From the Cocoon to a Butterfly

The isolation in everything you've suffered was your cocoon for transformation. It redefined your identity as you navigated your way through pain, fear and uncertainty. You discovered abilities, uncovered capacities and adapted to new realities. You're no longer a caterpillar but a beautiful butterfly. You've grown wings and have proven to be stronger than what was against you. The changes of your outer world forced a change of your inner being without your permission. You thought it would have broken you but it showed you that you were made for this. You built new muscles in places you didn't know existed. Your self-view has a new definition; faith and strength have been reformed!

She Declares

I declare that I walk in victory through our Lord Jesus Christ according to 1 Corinthians 15:57. I declare that I will have peace and overcome every roadblock according to John 16:33. I take courage as God repositions my life. I will spread my wings and soar!

She Meditates

Yet in all these things we are more than conquerors *and* gain an overwhelming victory through Him who loved us [so much that He died for us]. Romans 8:37 AMP

She Journals

~ DAY TWENTY-FOUR ~

Intimacy Reproduced

If you've made your request known unto God but haven't received it, you may begin to believe that faith probably doesn't work. Faith should not be positioned as a transaction where I believe so God can respond with my request. If that's the case, then we will become gods over God and that's not possible. We do not get to treat Him like a puppet. Faith is focused on God getting the glory, not on the request. When our expectations are focused on things and we do not receive them we begin to doubt God's power and care. At this point one is tempted to believe that faith doesn't work. Faith is relationship. Are you kind to others because you want the same in return or because being kind is a fruit of the spirit?

What have you been asking for and are your eyes fixed on the results or God's glory?

She Declares

I declare that I will diligently seek to give God glory in all I do. I decree and declare that I will please the LORD in my pursuit of Him. I declare that my faith is alive as I partnered with my actions. I decree that I am a mountain mover according to Mark 11:23.

She meditates

But without faith it is impossible to please Him: for he that cometh to God must believe that He is, and that He is a rewarder of them that diligently seek Him. Hebrews 11:6 KJV

She Journals

~ DAY TWENTY-FIVE ~

Confidently Confident

When you know who you are you'll see the gifts and talents of others through the eyes of collaboration instead of competition. You will not feel threatened by the presence of someone who walks boldly into the room. The need to fight for relevance will be nonexistent. Competing to prove you're better than others is an indication that you're unsure of your true value. When you know you are valuable, the need to make an announcement is never a priority. What's understood doesn't need to be explained.

It is time to do an inventory of the qualities you were created with, rebrand yourself and up your value. You are priceless and you need to know and believe it. Address every though of condemnation. Strive to be the splitting image of your heavenly Father.

She Declares

I am the righteousness of God according to 2 Corinthians 5:21. I conduct myself with integrity. I am an honorable woman and was created in God's image according to Genesis 1:27. I am royalty and God's special possession.

She meditates

But you are a chosen people, a royal priesthood, a holy nation, God's special possession, that you may declare the praises of him who called you out of darkness into His wonderful light. 1 Peter 2:9 NIV

She Journals

~ DAY TWENTY-SIX ~

Emotional Access

During the early years of our marriage, my husband and I were having a conversation. He mentioned that there were times when I made him angry but he ignored it to prevent any escalation. After he was finish speaking, I apologized. Then I said to him, "Baby whenever I make you angry, I would like for you to let me know." Why did I respond the way I did? First, because I needed to work on my contribution to his anger. As humans, we tend to pass on learned behaviors. We are to manage them and not deny them access. If they aren't expressed in one way, they will in another. The idea is to give your emotions the right to be processed. Address your feelings so you can control them instead of them controlling you. God gave us emotions to help us process and express life around us. Honor how you were created and embrace your emotions. There to tell you something is wrong and needs your attention.

She Declares

I am a woman with self-control. I conduct myself in a proper manner as I represent my Father and King. My words are seasoned with kindness and grace. My emotions do not control me but I control my emotions. Out of my heart flows love, joy, peace, kindness and gentleness. I am faithful.

She Meditates

Be ye angry and sin not: let not the sun go down upon your wrath.

Ephesians 4:26 KJV

She Journals

~ DAY TWENTY-SEVEN ~

Unveiling Love

God's love rescued me. It caused me to see the best version of me. It didn't remind me of how messy I was but affirmed me that I'm loved. That love motivated me to change. Now, I'm part of the 99. If you are the "one," know that God is after your heart. Remember, the scent of sin doesn't scare Him.

He is the one who will never leave the "one" behind. Without a care for the pain I've caused him, He came searching for me. I thought maybe I needed to be "good" before I could have earned His great affection. I reminded that I could never earn. I only needed to receive it because it's free. He left those who were safe and came looking for my endangered soul. He doesn't care how far you've gone. He wants to show you what true love looks like, save you and give you His peace. No distance is too far for Him to find you. He loves you without regard for his own heart. Yes, He will always leave the ninety-nine to come after you, the one. When you surrender to Him, He will celebrate you. He will forever love you – He's your Heavenly Father.

She Declares

I am a new creation. I am no longer a slave to sin. I am the apple of God's eyes. I am God's treasure. I am valuable. I am precious. I am strong. I am courageous and loved. I am enough. I am wealthy in love, knowledge and wisdom. I am saved.

She Meditates

This is how much God loved the world: He gave His Son, His one and only Son. And this is why: so that no one need be destroyed; by believing in Him, anyone can have a whole and lasting life. God didn't go to all the trouble of sending His Son merely to point an accusing finger, telling the world how bad it was. He came to help, to put the world right again. Anyone who trusts in Him is acquitted; anyone who refuses to trust Him has long since been under the death sentence without knowing it. John 3:16-18 MSG

She Journals

~ DAY TWENTY-EIGHT ~

Uncut Diamond

Diamonds are formed under the right pressure and temperature. You're not losing your mind...You're being formed.

Being so focused on the end results will result in you missing the lessons within the present moment. Destination addiction causes us to not trust God in the process. Yes, the process may hurt; look confusing, messy, undone, slow and even boring. It feels like pressure; that's because it is. Have you ever seen a diamond before it was processed? Would you wear it on your finger? It has to be processed before you can see it's true beauty.

Your time to sparkle is coming dear daughter. I know you see all the other diamonds shining brightly but stay focused over here and endure.

You're being made equipped for your next level, your next season. It looks dull because your process has not yet been completed. Get that good wisdom and remember the journey because they are going to need it when you walk into the room. In all your getting, get clarity.

She Declares

I will wait on God's timing for my strength to be renewed according to Isaiah 40:31. Though and hosts should encamp against me, my heart shall not fear according to Psalms 27:3. I will rise above every trial and allow my undone edges to be clipped. I will not be crushed neither will I be destroyed according to 2 Corinthians 4:8-9.

She Meditates

We are hard pressed on every side, but not crushed; perplexed, but not in despair; persecuted, but not abandoned; struck down, but not destroyed. 2 Corinthians 4: 8-9 NIV

She Journals

~ DAY TWENTY-NINE ~

Daddy's Girl

When your Father owns everything, you live everywhere and every day without limits. You are the direct image of your Heavenly Father. You are proof that releasing the things that pull at your heart and soul to God brings inner peace. It's the kind of peace that is beyond human reasoning.

You are proof that once you throw all your cares, worries, burdens to him, He will show you solutions. His desires are for you to conquer every satanic influence, break free from every generational shackle and operate with power, clarity and authority. He will heal you and elevate you above all fears. Check His track records, He has never lost a battle. His heart is beating for you. His eyes are turned towards you. You were meant to be the direct image of your Heavenly Father. You are your Daddy's girl.

She Declares

I am my Father's favorite. I've been made miraculously and amazingly by my Father's hands and I lack absolutely nothing. I AM AWESOME!

She Meditates

I will praise Thee; for I am fearfully and wonderfully made: marvelous are Thy works; and that my soul knoweth right well.

She Journals

~ DAY THIRTY ~

Pursuit of Purpose

As a queen within God's kingdom, you were created to make impact. Finding your purpose and walking in it is the pathway to reaching those you were called to.

1. What are you passionate about?
2. What is that specific thing you would still do even if you're not paid for it?
3. What breaks your heart and cause you to react?
4. What problems do you have solutions for?

One of the things that breaks my heart is when I see people live in poverty in relation to their God-given abilities. It stirs up a need and passion within me to help them discover the power they possess. I would willingly react by giving them the right information to become empowered and teach them mind elevation strategies.

Be diligent in finding your path in the kingdom and walk courageously in it.

She Declares

I will seek out who I am by seeking out who God is to me. I will take the time to uncover my passions and purpose. I am a problem solver. I partner with God to ensure the world has answers. I am an answer.

She Meditates

For if you remain silent at this time, relief and deliverance for the Jews will arise from another place, but you and your father's family will perish. And who knows but that you have come to your royal position for such a time as this? Esther 4:14 NIV

She Journals

~ DAY THIRTY-ONE ~

Delivered to Deliver

As you learn who you are and what you carry, the desire to locate those you are called to will emerge within. When you find your people, group or audience then you will be able to project what you carry towards them. Let your gifts make room for God's glory. Many are lost in various arenas of life but you are no longer one of them. The financial, relational, spiritual and professional realms need you. Whatever you've experienced and have mastered carries value. What do you value? When you merge your skills, achievements and experiences, you will produce solutions.

Be assured that you are a masterpiece! You are a pearl of great price! Lady, you are amazingly beautiful and your entrance into this new life of yours is welcomed with trumpets of glory. Walk in the greatness entrusted to you and do not be afraid to shine! This is the beginning of the rest of your life! *Hello Queen!*

She Declares

My presence creates a future for others. I am confident in what I've been called to do. I will be observant to the problems God has called me to find solutions. I was made for this and nothing will stop me.

She Meditates

I press on toward the goal to win the prize for which God has called me heavenward in Christ Jesus. Philippians 3:14 NIV

She Journals

FROM THE AUTHOR

I see your crown. Can you see it? You've made it to the end and I'm so proud of you. You are more powerful than you know. Your Heavenly Father has placed His love on you. The price of His love was the blood of Jesus, His only Son. He loved you enough to prove Himself by sending Jesus to die even though He knew no sin. Beloved, He loves you. Celebrate yourself for taking this journey of reminding yourself who you are and what you possess. Go on that wondrous journey to achieve all that God has in store for you. You are unstoppable! You are valuable. May the peace of God continue to surround you wherever you go and in all that you may do.

Your Queen in Christ,
Shirine McRae-Freeman

Made in the USA
Middletown, DE
30 April 2021